LIVING UNTIL JESUS COMES

Living

UNTIL
JESUS COMES

KAREN DOCKREY

VICTOR BOOKS®

A DIVISION OF SCRIPTURE PRESS PUBLICATIONS INC.
USA CANADA ENGLAND

Scripture quotations are from the *Holy Bible, New International Version* (NIV), © 1973, 1978, 1984, International Bible Society, used by permission of Zondervan Bible Publishers; and from J.B. Phillips: *The New Testament in Modern English*, Revised Edition (PH), © J.B. Phillips, 1958, 1960, 1972, permission of Macmillan Publishing Co. and Collins Publishers.

Recommended Dewey Decimal Classification: 227.81
Suggested Subject Heading: BIBLE, N.T.—PAULINE EPISTLES

Library of Congress Catalog Card Number: 88-62864
ISBN: 0-89693-668-6

VICTOR BOOKS A division of SP Publications, Inc. Wheaton, Illinois 60187

CONTENTS

The young Thessalonian Christians were intensely interested in the second coming of Jesus Christ. To answer their questions, Paul devoted a large portion of both Thessalonian letters to Jesus' return. However, Paul did not focus exclusively on the future. He addressed the Thessalonians' immediate worries, questions, and problems. They faced hostilities toward their faith, grief over dead loved ones, pressures to conform to the world's values, deceptive prophecies, and lazy people who wouldn't do their share.

Certainly a swift return of Jesus would have solved all the Thessalonians' problems. But that was not God's plan. Paul warned the Thessalonians not to let their excitement about Jesus' return distract them from God's present purposes. He indicated that the best way to express their excitement was to live for and learn from Jesus daily. This would lead to completeness in Christ.

Like the Thessalonians, we are curious about Jesus' second coming. We wonder if He will come in our lifetime. One of the best ways to express our eagerness for Jesus' return is to live for and learn from Him now. The Thessalonian letters contain discipleship principles that equip us to do exactly that. They might be subtitled: "Living Until Jesus Comes."

Examining the Background
It's not easy to understand one person's letter to another person unless you know a little something about those persons. In addition to the brief introduction above, you may want to peruse this more extensive introduction before studying 1 and 2 Thessalonians.

The church in Thessalonica was started by Paul while on his second missionary journey. The Jewish and Roman establishment were jealous of the young enthusiastic church and thus drove Paul from the city (Acts 17). He ended up in Corinth. Because Paul was forced to leave the Thessalonians suddenly, they had little leadership support as their faith grew. Thus, Paul sent Timothy to check on them. (Apparently

Timothy visiting was less offensive to Jewish leaders than Paul would have been.) When Timothy returned with a glowing report, Paul sent the first letter to the Thessalonians.

Some scholars believe that 1 Thessalonians was the first of Paul's biblical letters. He wrote 1 Thessalonians about A.D. 51 and the second letter about six months later.

Paul seemed to have a special fondness for the Thessalonians. Paul said he cared for them "like a mother caring for her little children" (1 Thes. 2:7). He was intensely concerned about their continuing persecution, their misunderstanding of the Lord's return, and the way they treated one another. He was proud that even in their tough situation, they continued to express their faith, persistence, and love.

In Paul's typical style, he began both letters by pointing out the areas in which the Thessalonian Christians were doing well, and then motivated them to do even better. His letters praised them, corrected them, instructed them, and encouraged them.

The situation in the church was similar for both letters. So the two letters are very similar. They both suggested ways to respond to persecution, assured the Thessalonians of Jesus' second coming, clarified misunderstandings about Jesus' return, encouraged spiritual growth, and promoted daily work. The first letter is warm and friendly; the second more formal, as though wanting to drive home points the Thessalonians didn't catch the first time.

Thessalonica was a busy seaport. It was an important communication and trade center with a population of about 200,000. It was the largest city in Macedonia and the capital of its province.

After becoming Christians, the Thessalonians learned more about Jesus through their struggles, worries, and problems. Jesus gave their daily routine new meaning and purpose. He gave them the ability to persevere when their loved ones died and when they were attacked for their faith. He taught them how to encourage and minister to each other. Learning from, living for, and growing closer to Jesus is called being a disciple. As Paul's words taught the Thessalonians to be disciples, they can do the same for us.

Using This Study Guide
This guide provides several ways to study and apply 1 and 2 Thessalonians:

  ☐ *Listening to the Bible:* This inductive Bible study is designed to help you listen to God's Word. Let the questions guide you in examining the Bible and drawing your own Spirit-led conclusions.

  ☐ *Life Examples:* This narrative section includes a story or informational article that shares one person's understanding of how to live the passage. If you are studying 1 and 2 Thessalonians in a group, underline as you read and share with your group the points you found most powerful. Star (★) points you want to ask questions about or discuss further.

☐ *Living until Jesus Comes:* The suggestions in this section are designed to help you apply the Bible truths to your daily life. Choose one or more that speaks to an area in which you need or want growth. Most will not be discussed during group study but feel free to do so if you find it beneficial. Feel free to adapt them as they best meet your needs.

☐ *Learning from Others:* At the back of the book are leader's guide suggestions that can deepen your own personal study or equip you to lead others in the study of 1 and 2 Thessalonians. Complete the above three sections before coming to group study.

CHAPTER ONE

MODEL YOUR

❦ *LISTENING TO GOD'S WORD* ❦

Waiting for Jesus' return can be both exciting and frustrating. While urging believers to look for Christ, Paul emphasized that they not neglect their daily spiritual commitment. Paul encouraged the Thessalonians to demonstrate their beliefs through what they did and said. He pointed out the many ways they were already doing this and expressed thankfulness to God for the faith and love they demonstrated. As you study this passage, think about the way Christians have modeled Christ for you and how your life might model Christ for others.

Read 1 Thessalonians 1:1-10

1. Examine Acts 17:1-9 to discover the beginning of the Thessalonian church. What facts impress you most firmly?

   What problems did the Thessalonians' beginning create?

2. Paul used the typical letter form of his day. Find these portions in verse 1:

   The author(s) of the letter—

10

The recipient of the letter—

The greeting—

3. Next in first-century letter form came a prayer of gratitude. For what was Paul grateful? (vv. 2-3)

   How do memories of you affect your friends? How have you encouraged them, frustrated them, worried them, inspired them?

4. True faith expresses itself through action. How did the Thessalonians exhibit this? (vv. 3-5ff)

   With what similar actions and words do you express your faith?

5. What suffering (v. 6) did the Thessalonians experience according to Acts 17:1-15?

What do you think gave them courage to believe even under these circumstances?

6. In your opinion, which of the Thessalonians' actions and attitudes was Paul commending as a "model to all the believers"? (v. 7)

Name a believer who is a model of Christian living for you. What actions (or attitudes) make her a model?

7. Name several differences between God and idols (v. 9).

8. Turning "to God from idols" illustrates repentance. How did repentance change the Thessalonians' lives? (vv. 6-10)

How has repentance changed your life?

9. Verse 10 is packed with important truths about Jesus. Name these and then circle the one that means the most to you. Why did you choose the one you did?

For Further Study: Study the greetings in Paul's letters by reading the first few verses of each of Paul's letters. What words are repeated again and again? Why do you think Paul emphasized the words he did? How are the greetings in 1 and 2 Thessalonians similar to Paul's other greetings? How are they different?

🐚 LIFE EXAMPLES 🐚

When I think of faithful people I think of Nancy, David, Earl, and Marlene. In their own unique ways they demonstrate Christ to me. Nancy believed in me when I was a teenager and told me so. She wrote letters encouraging me. She always gave me smiles and positive words. When I had no confidence in myself, she assured me I could live my faith. Nancy models Jesus.

David became my friend when I was a young adult. His keen grasp of spiritual truth and his clear way of communicating demonstrated how right God's truth is. He listened when I or my husband needed him. He came to us when he needed encouragement. We understood each other and stood by each other. David models Jesus.

Earl models Jesus to my young daughters. As a teacher of three-year-olds in our church, he takes time to listen to the concerns and celebrations of each one. He knows the questions to ask to help them feel comfortable, the words to use to help them understand Jesus. He speaks to each child by name whenever he sees them. Church is a happy place for children because of Earl. Earl models Jesus.

Marlene teaches junior high youth with me in Sunday School. She sees the best in each teenager and tells them what she sees: "Hey, you look great today!" "I like the way you answered that question." "Can I come by your house and pester you tomorrow night?" The girls believe Jesus loves them because they know Marlene loves them. Marlene models Jesus.

What does it mean to be a model of faith? Modeling has two facets:

☐ Choosing Christian people to imitate (1 Thes. 1:4-6).
☐ Being the kind of Christian others want to imitate (1 Thes. 1:7-10).

Use the following acrostic to recognize Christian models and recall actions to model in your own life.

M ention each other in your prayers (v. 2).
O ur Lord Jesus Christ gives hope that enables us to endure (v. 3).
D eep conviction motivates us to express God's power (v. 5).
E xpress joy in spite of suffering (v. 6).
L et the Lord's message ring out in your life (v. 7).

G ive a warm reception to each other (v. 8).
O mit idols to serve God (v. 9).
D efinitely wait for Jesus (v. 10).

Whom do you model your life after? Who models their lives after you? In 1 Corinthians 11:1 Paul urged his readers to be imitators of him as he is of Christ. Choose to imitate those who imitate Christ. Be like Christ so those who admire you will become like Christ. Jot down your three favorite ways to do this, rereading 1 Thessalonians 1:1-10 for ideas.

❧ *LIVING UNTIL JESUS COMES* ❧

Memorize 1 Thessalonians 1:7 to remind yourself to be a model of
Christian living.

****

Select at least two people who have been models of Christian living
for you (v. 7). Write a letter to each telling specifically how he or she
has helped you grow in Christ. Mail or hand-deliver the letters.

****

Idol worship was popular in the Thessalonians' day. Today we
worship such idols as money, success, position, and possessions. Using
clay or foil, shape an idol you tend to depend on. Display it where you
will see it daily as a reminder that God has much more power, and as a
reminder not to worship idols (v. 9).

****

Tell or write about a time you experienced joy in the Lord in spite of
severe suffering (v. 6).

CHAPTER TWO

Respond

TO YOUR MINISTERS

❧ LISTENING TO GOD'S WORD ❧

When a minister becomes involved in scandal or takes advantage of his church, it casts doubt on all ministers. We Christians need to examine each minister individually, knowing that one bad apple doesn't spoil the whole bunch. Paul encouraged the Thessalonians to scrutinize him. He was one good apple among a bunch of bad ones. Those bad apples had apparently spread rumors questioning Paul's character and the sincerity of his ministry. Paul urged the Thessalonians to depend on what they knew.

Read 1 Thessalonians 2:1-16
1. What criticisms do you suppose people had leveled against Paul, according to verses 3-12?

2. Name several phrases in 1 Thessalonians 2:1-12 that demonstrate that Paul's visit was not a failure and that his critics had no ground for their accusations.

3. Paul had battled both physical hardships and insults to his character and ministry (v. 2; cp. Acts 16:16—17:15). Which do you think would have been most discouraging to him? Why?

Who had inflicted suffering on the Thessalonians? (v. 14)

The Thessalonians' sufferings were no minor battles, but major physical and spiritual ordeals. How do you think Paul and the Thessalonians obeyed God "in spite of opposition"? (vv. 2, 13-15)

4. Repeatedly Paul relied on the Thessalonians' testimony about him and his ministry. They knew the truth about him, no matter what others said. What evidence do you see of this in:

Verse 1—

Verse 5—

Verse 9—

Verse 10—

Verse 11—

5. Reread verses 6-8 and 10-12. How would you describe Paul's leadership style?

6. In Paul's day it was customary for traveling missionaries to be housed and fed by church members. Why do you think Paul worked long hours as a tentmaker to support himself? (v. 9; cp. Acts 18:3)

7. Paul compared his ministry to the roles of a mother (vv. 7-8) and a father (vv. 11-12). What characteristics of each were demonstrated in Paul's ministry?

Mother   *Father*

8. Unlike their neighbors, the Thessalonians recognized Paul's teachings as the Word of God (v. 13). How do you think they told the difference between God's Word and the word of men?

How do you tell the difference?

9. The Jews were committed religious people who apparently meant well. Why do you think they displeased God and acted hostilely toward people? (vv. 15-16)

10. "Wrath of God" has been defined as letting people have the consequences of their sins. How do verses 15-16 support this definition?

Name a consequence of these sins that demonstrates this definition:

Gossip—

Unresolved anger—

Criticism—

11. Who in your church do you want to imitate? Why?

How does the person you choose to imitate demonstrate what you believe? (vv. 13-14)

For Further Study: Examine Paul's leadership style by reading Acts 13–21. Jot down phrases that describe his leadership style and the ways he taught about Jesus. Notice how what he says about himself in 1 Thessalonians 2 matches his actions recorded in Acts.

❦ LIFE EXAMPLES ❦

Sexual scandal. It's not something we expect to find connected with church leaders. But not long ago two well-known television evangelists became even better known for their sexual sins. When the affairs became public, the whole world noticed. Both Christians and non-Christians became suspicious of television preachers. Many became skeptical of Christianity as a whole. Those who had resisted Christianity used the scandals to prove their point.

Financial gain. It's not a goal we want our ministers to strive for. Even so, questionable money practices plague some ministers and churches. Some preachers insist that giving to their ministry will increase your personal wealth. Those same preachers don't mind enjoying the personal wealth that results from your giving. Other pastors quietly pilfer the offering plate. Part of the problem may be the poor salaries we pay—the pastor may not have enough to pay his bills. Whether for understandable reasons or not, some ministers have trouble overcoming the greed that accompanies human nature.

Do these incidents mean that all pastors and ministers are to be regarded with suspicion? Certainly not. But we do need to evaluate each one. Paul suggested in 1 Thessalonians 2 that we depend on what we know and witness. The Greek verb translated "know" means to know with certainty, to understand from personal experience. Rather than depending on what someone else says or on your feelings at the moment, think back through your experiences with your pastor or other church leader. Have you experienced a minister who teaches falsehood, acts power-hungry, or otherwise demonstrates ungodliness? Have you experienced a genuine and godly pastor who makes mistakes but does well most of the time? Evaluate your pastor in the light of the Bible.

What qualified Paul to advise us on this matter? Paul was the victim of rumors which said he was just like all the other religious teachers and philosophers of his day. Religious teachers around him were known for their dishonesty and deception. They took advantage of people's trust to gain fame and fortune. Rather than speaking for God, they said and did whatever brought them personal gain. Other religions promoted temple prostitution. "Believers" were taught that they could come close to their god by uniting (sexually) with the god's "consecrated ones."

Paul denied any connection with such outrageous behavior. He appealed to the Thessalonians' experience with him. His behavior provided evidence that he was not like all the rest. While with the Thessalonians he had demonstrated sincerity, moral uprightness, godly teaching and love. He did not seek their money, nor did he promote immoral sexual practices (vv. 3-6). He loved them as a true mother (vv. 7-8) and a father would (vv. 11-12).

Reread 1 Thessalonians 1:1-16. Paul's actions demonstrated genuine ministerial characteristics such as:

☐ Telling the Gospel (v. 2)
☐ Not trying to trick anyone (v. 3)
☐ Letting God examine inner motives and outer actions (vv. 4-6)
☐ Never using flattery or greed (v. 5)
☐ Gentleness (v. 7)
☐ Care (v. 7)
☐ Sharing of life with the church (v. 8)
☐ Working long hours (v. 9)
☐ Encouraging (v. 12)
☐ Comforting (v. 12)
☐ Urging to live godly lives (v. 13)

Which of these qualities do your leaders demonstrate? The Thessalonians had heard criticisms of Paul. He encouraged them to evaluate these criticisms against their experiences with him. What criticisms have you heard about your pastor or other ministers? Which are true? If you see evidence of fraud, find an authentic leader who can help you decide what to do about it. When, as is often the case, you see genuine ministry, take action to show you notice and appreciate your minister:

☐ Become as open with compliments as complaints. Tell your leaders (and other people) what you see. Your positive regard can cut down on criticism and promote church unity.

☐ Write a note that says "I appreciate you."

☐ Restate to him something from a message or ministry that has helped you or someone you care about (rather than saying, "I liked your message").

☐ Watch his actions and notice how they support his calling. Tell him what you see.

☐ Recognize and accept God's Word.
☐ Live the Word of God through service, relationships, and routine (v. 14).

As these last two suggestions state, living until Jesus comes includes living God's Word. Often God communicates His Word through our leaders. Choose to recognize and live the truth your leaders teach:

> And we also thank God continually because, when you received the Word of God, which you heard from us, you accepted it not as the word of men, but as it actually is, the Word of God, which is at work in you who believe.
>
> —1 Thessalonians 2:13

❦*LIVING UNTIL JESUS COMES*❦

Memorize 1 Thessalonians 2:11-12. Ponder ways your pastor or other church leader does this for you. Jot down ways you might do these for others.

****

Put yourself in a Thessalonian Christian's shoes. Imagine you have been through personal suffering and your leader has been questioned by prominent religious people. Which statements in 1 Thessalonians 2:1-16 would have given you the greatest assurance?

****

Write a letter to your pastor, noting his sincerity and specific ways he has ministered to you.

****

Privately jot down several criticisms you have of your pastor or church leader. Now write two compliments for each criticism. How does focusing on the good help both you and your minister?

CHAPTER THREE

Encourage

DURING SEPARATION

❧ *LISTENING TO GOD'S WORD* ❧

Whom do you miss? A husband away on business? A parent who has died? A child away at college? A friend or family member who lives a long distance from you? Paul and the Thessalonians were separated and missed each other desperately. As you study this passage, notice words, actions, and attitudes of Paul's that made the distance less painful.

Read 1 Thessalonians 2:17–3:13

1. Paul was torn from the Thessalonians by an angry group of Jews (2:17). Read Acts 17:1-10, putting yourself in the shoes of one of the Jews who had become a believer. How would you have responded to Paul's departure?

Read Acts 17:1-15, imagining you were one of the jealous Jews who wanted Paul out of town. Why did you want him to leave? How did you feel when he preached somewhere else?

Read Acts 17:1-10 again, imagining you are Paul. What feelings do you have? What actions would you want to take? How would God have helped you through this crisis?

2. Jot down phrases from 1 Thessalonians 2:17-19 that support your answers about Paul in the previous question. How correct were you in imagining what Paul felt about his separation from the Thessalonians?

3. How do other Christians serve as "our hope, our joy, our crown" in which we glory? (v. 19)

   Name and describe at least one person who does this for you.

4. Describe the details concerning the actions Paul took to ease the pain of separation (3:1-5):

   The person Paul sent—

   This person's role with Paul—

   What Paul wanted this person to do for the Thessalonians—

Why Paul sent him—

5. What role do you think "the tempter" (Satan) plays in persecutions? (vv. 3-5)

6. How did Paul respond to Timothy's news about the Thessalonian church? Write phrases from verses 6-10 that support your answer:

   Now dig further by circling all the words that describe thanksgiving and joy, and underlining the personal pronouns "you" and "we." (These communicated the oneness Paul feels with the Thessalonians.)

7. Reread verse 6. How does faith contribute to love, and love contribute to faith?

8. "Distress and persecution" in verse 7 describe both spiritual·anguish and physical suffering. Write specific words or actions you could take to help a fellow Christian through one or both of these types of pain, based on these principles from verses 6-11:

Share good news and/or good memories (v. 6)—

Live your faith (v. 7)—

Stand firm in the Lord (v. 8)—

Give each other joy (v. 9)—

Pray for each other and actually get together (v. 10)—

Supply what is lacking in each other's faith (v. 11)—

9. Describe Paul's threefold blessing in verses 11-13.

   Which part of the blessing would you most like to receive? To give?

10. "Heart" (v. 13) refers to the whole of the inner life. How do you express your God-given strength and holiness through these parts of your inner life:

    Decisions—

    Intentions—

Thoughts—

Motives—

Plans—

11. Reread the blessing in verses 11-13 substituting your name for every "you" and "your."

For Further Study: Read 2 Timothy to discover more about Paul's later relationship with Timothy and Paul's ministry instructions for Timothy.

Imagine how Timothy would have helped you if he had visited you. Then ponder ways you could grant the same kind of encouragement to another Christian you know.

🍂 *LIFE EXAMPLES* 🍂

First Thessalonians 2:17–3:13 suggests several actions to take during times of separation:

☐ Focus on Christ's return (2:19; 3:13)
☐ Say that you think of the other often (2:17)
☐ Make effort to see each other (2:17-19; 3:10-11)
☐ Contact a friend who can be with them (3:1-2)
☐ Encourage each other during trials, helping each other grow closer to God, not further from Him (3:3-5)
☐ Share memories (3:6)
☐ Tell expressions of faith that you notice in each other (3:7)
☐ Thank God for each other, naming specific joys received (3:9)
☐ Encourage each other's love and strength (3:12-13)

Underline phrases in the following letter that express one or more of the above actions:

My dear Rita,

I don't believe I've ever had a friend like you. You listen to me, understand me, encourage me, motivate me, and make me feel competent and so totally loved. I think of you often and worry about you when you're going through hard times. As you face your surgery, you might want to contact Mary. She lives in your town and has been through it herself. She said she'd be glad to answer your questions. I know it's scary but I also know God is right by your side, going with you through it all. His love and strength will bring you through. I wish I could be there in person. I'll definitely be with you in thought and prayer.

I look forward to next summer when we can get together. I hope to call soon after your surgery to talk about the results and to plan our reunion. I can hardly wait for our children to meet each other.

When I think about you, my heart warms. I love the way you talk about your faith in such a natural, unpreachy style. I tend to freeze up when it comes to talking about God, but He's as natural for you as talking about the weather. It's so obvious that you let Him help with your marriage and the way you parent. You really are faith in action. You've given me joy by helping faith become a natural part of me, by considering my ideas important, by always understanding. You've strengthened my faith like no one but the Lord Himself.

I look forward to heaven where we'll never have to be separated again!

Your friend,
Diane

❧ *LIVING UNTIL JESUS COMES* ❧

Memorize 1 Thessalonians 3:13 as a reminder that true faith is based on God's strength and is lived out in daily decisions.

******

Name someone who gives you hope, joy, and victory (2:19-20). Write a blessing for him or her similar to the one in verses 3:11-13. Use these words in your blessing: "God," "love," "strength," "Lord Jesus comes."

******

Write phrases people have said during a separation that *don't* help or that make you feel worse. Translate these into helpful phrases/actions.

******

Read 1 Thessalonians 2:17–3:13 several times. As you read it underline words, actions, and attitudes Paul used to deal with his separation from the Thessalonians. Which do you think were most helpful to the Thessalonians? Which might have been more helpful to Paul? Which help you most in dealing with separation?

******

One day we'll no longer have to experience separation from loved ones. Read verse 2:19 and 3:13. Write yourself a brief letter about how Jesus' coming changes the way you view your present longings (2:17-19; 3:6-11).

CHAPTER FOUR

GOD DAILY

❧ LISTENING TO GOD'S WORD ❧

What could you do to please God? Become a missionary to Africa? Win a thousand souls to Christ? Give all your money away? Certainly God would be impressed by such dramatic sacrifice. Or would He? In 1 Thessalonians 4, Paul discussed how to please God in less dramatic but equally important ways. Paul stressed daily obedience in such areas as sex, interpersonal relationships, and work. God calls for daily devotion.

Daily obedience sounds so insignificant, so humdrum. But God recognizes its excitement. He knows the adventure we will encounter when we obey Him day by day, experience by experience. God understands that these little things add up to big things and that when we obey Him daily, we become more responsive to His leadership in our major decisions. Major on the minors. In Christianity, it works.

Read 1 Thessalonians 4:1-12
1. Think about your daily routine. Name several ways you could exhibit devotion to God in the course of this daily routine. Include at least one action you already do.

2. Reread 1 Thessalonians 4:3-4. Why do you think sexual sins are some of the hardest to resist?

3. God's commands for our sex lives have very positive roots. He's as interested in what we do as what we don't do. Paraphrase each of the commands in verses 3-8 without "no," "not," or "don't" to emphasize their positiveness.

4. Name at least three reasons to refrain from sex outside of marriage (vv. 5-7).

5. The Phillips translation of verse 6 says, "You cannot break this rule without cheating and exploiting your fellow-men." Give several examples of pain caused by premarital and extramarital sex.

6. *Holy* means "dedicated to God" or "set apart for God." How does sex within marriage demonstrate holy living? (v. 7)

   How would you describe the excitement of living in sexual holiness (v. 7) to someone who thinks sexual loyalty is old-fashioned?

7. "That's okay if it works for you. It's just not right for me," argue some who reject God's sexual standards. How do we know that God's Word demands obedience from everyone? (v. 8)

How would you respond to someone who said this statement?

8. "Brotherly love" describes the love between children of the same father. What demonstrations of brotherly love do you see among your church or fellowship group? (vv. 9-10)

What examples of "sibling rivalry" have you seen in your church or Bible study group?

What steps might you take to make your love more powerful than your rivalry?

9. How would every person working at a significant task discourage nosiness and laziness? (v. 11) What might this task be for you?

10. What's the difference between a "quiet life" (v. 11) and a reclusive life?

11. Think of a non-Christian you know. With what daily-life actions could you win his/her respect? (v. 12)

How might this respect become openness to God?

For Further Study: Study the word *sanctified* (1 Thes. 4:3) in these three ways:

1—Look up *sanctify* in a Bible dictionary. Write out a definition in your own words.

2—Read several Bible verses in which *sanctify, sanctified,* or *sanctification* occur. Discover these with a Bible concordance.

3—Explain *sanctification* as though you are speaking to someone with little or no church experience.

&LIFE EXAMPLES &

Rebekkah's marriage had become routine at best. Her husband Gene worked long hours while she spent many lonely evenings at home. She found her thoughts wandering to Russell, a former boyfriend. Why hadn't she married him? He was romantic. He had written love poem after love poem for her. She reviewed the words to the poems he had written. Certainly he would see her as more important than his job. Why hadn't she recognized his love when she had it? Why hadn't she responded to his hopes for their future? How marvelous their life together would have been!

For several weeks these thoughts persisted. Rebekkah became obsessed with the idea of contacting Russell. Perhaps he too was unhappy in his marriage. Maybe talking would help both of them. She composed several letters to him but couldn't bring herself to mail them.

At night she dreamed about their reunion but found herself troubled by the dream's ending. When she appeared on Russell's doorstep, Russell put his arm around his wife and said, "But why are you here? We're very happy together." Rebekkah reluctantly admitted that the dream and her resistance to mailing the letters might be messages from God—gentle nudges toward reality.

She read a columnist's response to a question similar to hers: "Did I marry the wrong person?" The columnist suggested that one reason we return to thoughts of a previous sweetheart is that we've never had to go through real life with him. No midnight feedings, no trouble with in-laws, no all-night stomach flu, no money problems. These problems gnaw away at romance and force us to develop mature love. It's not as gushy but it's definitely longer-lasting. The columnist explained that day-to-day living is seldom romantic but can always be loving.

Rebekkah recognized her thoughts as a type of mental adultery. She was betraying Gene with her thoughts just as definitely as if she had slept with Russell. But she couldn't control her thoughts; they just popped into her head. Or could she?

She began to realize that she had selected only her happy memories of Russell. And she had selected only her frustrations with Gene. She forced herself to recall the frustrations she had had with Russell and the pleasures that had convinced her that Gene was right for her. Just as she had noticed the things Russell had that Gene lacked, she deliberately focused on the things she would miss about Gene if she had married Russell. She realized that no one person could have every quality she might want in a spouse. Fortunately, Gene had most of them. She had become so centered on what Gene lacked that she became blind to what he had. She noticed in a fresh way his ability to bring out the best in her, his encouragement, his handsomeness.

Rebekkah gradually grew a renewed love for Gene. She confessed her feelings of disloyalty and her frustration with his lack of romance. She shared with him all the good qualities she had rerecognized as a result of her struggle. She reviewed with him the ways they had grown close over the years. She vowed to cultivate even deeper love as they worked through their frustrations. She reaffirmed the truth of Matthew 19:5: "For this reason a man will leave his father and mother and be united to his wife, and the two will become one flesh." Though the transformation wasn't instantaneous, and though Gene never did write love poems, Rebekkah found herself most delightfully in love with him.

Rebekkah's battle to delight God and delight in her husband was a silent one. But it was just as powerful as any outward transformation. She discovered that God's way of loving works, that the best relationships are carved day by day, problem by problem, joy by joy. She realized that the world's encouragement to "try someone new when the old one gets boring" just doesn't work. She noticed that letting Gene know her relationship needs encouraged the two of them to outdo each other in demonstrating love. And she rekindled the fire that had originally brought them together.

First Thessalonians 4:1-12 guides us to obey in the everyday relationships: marriage, sexuality, friendships, work. Notice the truths that encourage you to delight God daily.

❧*LIVING UNTIL JESUS COMES*❧

Memorize 1 Thessalonians 4:1 or 4:9. As you encounter people this week, think about how you can please God through your relationship with each person.

****

If you are married, write at least twenty qualities you enjoy or appreciate about your husband. Circle the three you would most miss if you were no longer married. Commit to tell your husband daily something you appreciate about him. Notice how your love life grows.

If you are not married, write at least ten advantages of God's plan for sex and ten ways you fit into His plan. Thank God for His good plan. Notice ways He meets your need for love.

****

Think about a friend who means a great deal to you. Read 1 Thessalonians 4:9-10. What loving actions come naturally in your relationship? (v. 9) What loving actions do you have to work at? (v. 10) Commit to continue building this relationship.

****

Choose a verse from 1 Thessalonians 4:1-12 to illustrate. Don't fret if you have little artistic talent—stick figures are fine. Visualizing God's Word helps settle it in our minds.

CHAPTER FIVE

GOD'S WAY

☙LISTENING TO GOD'S WORD❧

"Don't cry. He's better off now. Just think: He's with God! As Christians we don't have to grieve when our loved ones die! We rejoice!" said Gina.

"That sounds good," responded Beverly, "but I can't get my feelings to agree. Certainly I'm glad Michael is with God, but I still miss him. Some days I feel so empty and sad that I can hardly move. I've lost my husband, and my children have lost their daddy. How can my tears be wrong? It's not that I don't trust God. I trust Him now more than ever. He's the one helping me through my pain. He's the one who gives me hope."

Read 1 Thessalonians 4:13-18

1. What's the difference between grieving without hope and grieving with hope? (v. 13)

What advice might Paul give to Beverly? (vv. 13-18)

2. Reread verse 13. Paul realized that knowledge takes away fear. Thus he did not want the Thessalonians "to be ignorant" about those who had died. What truths in 1 Thessalonians 4:13-18 ease your fear about your own death or a loved one's death?

3. The phrase "fall asleep" in verses 13-15 is a euphemism referring to death. Yet dead Christians really will wake up again. How and when? (vv. 16-18)

4. Paul did not discourage the Thessalonians from grieving. Rather he encouraged them to grieve with hope. What is the Christian's hope? (vv. 14, 16-17; read 1 Corinthians 15:12-20 for a more detailed explanation of verse 14.)

   How does Jesus' resurrection guarantee that this hope will come true?

5. Why do you think Paul used the phrase "according to the Lord's own word" in verse 15?

6. "Caught up together with them" (v. 17) describes our reunion with those who have died. Who do you most want to see when Jesus returns? What do you want to say when you see him/her again?

7. Imagine the Lord's return as detailed in verses 16-17. What colors, sounds, and feelings do you think you will see, hear, and experience? Draw or write your image:

8. According to verse 17 we will "be with the Lord forever." How would you explain this benefit to someone who is not a Christian?

9. Verse 18 instructs us to encourage ("comfort" in some translations) one another with these words. What words from this passage would you use to comfort and encourage a friend grieving over a dead loved one? (v. 18)

10. Beverly will face new problems because her husband has died. She will raise her young children alone and double many other daily responsibilities. How can focusing on Jesus' second coming make her day-to-day problems more manageable?

For Further Study: Read Granger Westberg's *Good Grief* (Fortress) for deeper understanding of the grief process.

❧ *LIFE EXAMPLES* ❧

Most of us shy away from the hard questions and troublesome experiences of life. "Don't think about it. Just keep busy," we tell ourselves and others. Death is one of these hard experiences. Fortunately for all Christians, Paul refused to ignore the hard questions. His Thessalonian brothers and sisters worried about their loved ones who had died. Apparently they had misunderstood Paul's teaching and thought all believers would live until Jesus' return. When believing friends and relatives died and Jesus hadn't returned, those still living became confused. Would their dead loved ones miss out on Jesus' return? Paul addressed their confusion with truth. He knew that accurate understanding of the second coming of Christ would prevent worry and bring peace.

Paul assured the Thessalonians that those who died would not miss out on Jesus' second coming. In fact, they would rise to meet Him first. Living believers would then join them for a most joyous reunion.

Until Jesus returns, believers will die and those left behind will miss them. Paul explained that this grief is different from that of a non-Christian. The difference is hope. First Thessalonians 4:13 can be translated, "As you are grieving remember the hope of Christ."

What does it mean to grieve with hope? The pain of losing someone by death is similar whether you are a Christian or not. But we Christians know that we will see our loved ones again, that death is not the end. Non-Christians see nothing beyond the grave; they have no hope. The certainty of Jesus' return and our reunion with family and friends makes a Christian's grief less devastating.

Pastors who walk through grief with their parishioners explain grief as "thinking about the dead loved one and letting ourselves feel the loss." Too often we "get busy" and refuse to allow ourselves time to think, to feel, to talk about the death. We fear that sadness is somehow unchristian. But recall Jesus' sadness after the death of His dear friend

Lazarus (John 11:32-36). Onlookers recognized Jesus' tears as a demonstration of His love for Lazarus.

Isn't it selfish to grieve when we know they're happy being with Jesus? No, it's not selfish. It's smart. Of course we're happy that our loved ones are with Jesus. We're happy that one day we'll join them. These are exactly the hopes that get us through our sadness. But while we're waiting to see them again, we miss them. We call this missing "grief" and we express it through tears, words, and feelings. As we tell Jesus and Christian friends how much we miss our loved one, and how grateful we are that she touched our lives, we begin to feel better. When we let ourselves cry and give ourselves extra rest, we experience renewal. Jesus heals our sadness, both at the time of death and when He returns. He assures us that He will be back and all will be fine. Our sadness doesn't end in despair.

Many illustrate grieving as letting a cut bleed. When we cut a finger, our first impulse is to cover it—to stop the bleeding. But our mothers taught us, and medical science confirms, that letting it bleed awhile aids healing. Bleeding washes out impurities that, if closed in, would result in infection. Soap and water add to the body's natural cleansing. After bleeding and cleansing, we bandage the wound carefully so that scarring won't occur.

In the same way, when we lose a loved one by death, part of us is cut away. The closer the person was to us, the greater the pain. Letting our emotions bleed and accepting the cleansing care of loved ones and friends enables our loss to heal rather than fester. We can close the wound without scars.

Grief comes in several stages and has several characteristics:

☐ *Shock.* Initially, most of us feel numb. We wonder why we can't cry or don't feel. Does this mean that we didn't love them? Of course not. Quite to the contrary, we're feeling so much that our system gives us some time off.

☐ *Strong Feelings.* Following or mingled with the shock, comes extreme sadness. Many cry; others sigh; several simply feel hopeless and depressed. Many grieving persons go through a period of anger and guilt. We feel angry at God, the doctors, or even the loved one for dying. These feelings can make us feel guilty. Rather than feeling guilty, we can talk with God about them. God can handle our anger; He understands the pain behind it and offers His healing love. We might regret something we did or failed to do; something we said or failed to say. Confession and talking bring forgiveness and renewal.

☐ *Acceptance.* Finally we feel ready to go on with life. We continue to miss the person but feel like ourselves again. We can concentrate on the joy of seeing them again rather than mourning their loss. It can take up to a year to reach this point.

Is it worth it to contribute so much time to grief? Doesn't giving in to these feelings indicate weakness or lack of trust? Not at all. In fact, we usually do ourselves more harm than good when we ignore our feelings. Remember the cut: holding in feelings causes infection. Feelings are a part of the good way God created us. When we let ourselves grieve or listen to friends as they grieve, we obey Ecclesiastes 3:1, 4: "There is a time for everything . . . a time to weep and a time to laugh, a time to mourn and a time to dance."

Focusing on the splendor of Jesus' return gives us hope even when we aren't grieving. After reading 1 Thessalonians 4:15-17, many of us respond with questions like: "Where are the dead when they meet Jesus?" "Are they already with Him in heaven?" "How long will it be before those alive join them?" "When will the Lord return?" The answers to these questions are not presented in this passage, likely because its purpose is encouragement, not chronology. And the answers may be beyond our understanding: heaven and our reunion with Jesus will be dramatically different from anything we've ever experienced. Even so, it can be a worship experience to imagine it. What do you imagine Jesus' second coming will be like? What will you say and do? Whom are you most anxious to see?

Though we may not understand all the details, we do know that Jesus will return. We can leave the details to Him while we enjoy the security of resting in His care.

❦*LIVING UNTIL JESUS COMES*❦

Memorize 1 Thessalonians 4:13-14 to help you remember the certainty of your hope in Christ.

****

Think about a loved one who has died. How does your faith in Jesus affect how you feel about his/her death? Take a moment to grieve over this special someone who has died. Write or ponder your thoughts. What truths in 1 Thessalonians 4:13-18 give you encouragement?

****

Who do you know who has recently experienced the death or serious illness of a loved one? Call that friend and offer your time to listen, to help with housework, to care for children, to cover church responsibilities. Realize that your listening is valuable ministry—it's very difficult to find someone who will listen to sad experiences. Ask questions like:
☐ What do you miss most about him?
☐ He certainly was special. I remember _____ . What do you remember?
☐ I'd like to give you an hour of my time. How would you like to use it? (Better than "Call me if I can do anything.")
Sometimes grieving friends don't want words as much as they want presence. What actions would encourage your friend?

****

Jesus' return is certain. Write a letter to a friend or to Jesus telling how this truth helps you enjoy life. Include ways Jesus' return takes the fear out of death as well as giving depth to present events.

 FOR JESUS

❧LISTENING TO GOD'S WORD❧

When is Jesus coming back? Believers have wondered this since He left the first time. Many, convinced that they know the date of His arrival, produce elaborate charts and checklists of events leading to "the Day of the Lord." Paul explained that the times and dates are not nearly as important as the way we live day by day. Discover ways to live as a child of the light as you wait for Jesus.

Read 1 Thessalonians 5:1-11

1. What question had the Thessalonians asked, according to 5:1?

2. Rather than times and dates, Paul gave the Thessalonians encouragement. Find evidence of this in verses 1-11. Jot down what you find.

3. Describe the way a "thief in the night" comes (v. 2).

4. Why do you think people will think things are peaceful and safe when they are not? (v. 3)

Do you think these falsely secure people will be believers or non-believers? Why?

5. The key word in verse 4 is probably "surprise." Explain why.

6. Believers are described as "sons of light" and "sons of the day" in verse 5. Describe the difference between a son of light/day and a son of darkness/night. Include actions, attitudes, and appearance (vv. 5-7).

7. Describe someone who is going through the motions of life but is really "asleep" (v. 6). Don't mention any names (your "person" might be a composite of several people you know).

8. Using a Bible dictionary or by reading verses 6-8 in several Bible translations, define "self-controlled" (sometimes translated "sober").

Name one way you could express self-control in these areas and so demonstrate your standing as a child of the light (vv. 6, 8):

Family relationships—

Church participation—

Job—

Neighborhood—

Private life—

9. Why do you think faith and love are compared to a breastplate? (v. 8)

   How is salvation like a helmet? (v. 8)

10. Salvation has both a negative side (avoiding wrath, v. 9) and a positive side (living with God forever, v. 10). Which would you rather emphasize? Why?

11. Describe or doodle your thoughts and feelings about being with God whether alive or dead (vv. 9-10).

12. Write something encouraging about every person in your Bible study group (v. 11). When you meet, tell each what you wrote.

13. Several of the Thessalonian Christians were apparently anxious about their own salvation. Which verse or verses in 1 Thessalonians 5:1-11 do you think would most assure them of their security in Christ?

For Further Study: Look up the word *light* in a Bible concordance. Read every reference from your Bible, including the verses around it. Based on what you have read, write a definition of the way *light* is used in the Bible. Reread 1 Thessalonians 5:1-11 enhanced with your new insight.

Following the same procedure, study the phrase "Day of the Lord."

❧ LIFE EXAMPLES ❧

As you read this prayer based on 1 Thessalonians 5:1-11, underline thoughts or feelings you have had. Jot in the margin other thoughts about Jesus' second coming.

Lord, when that speaker asked me if I was a premillennialist, postmillennialist, or amillennialist, I didn't know what to say. I don't even know what those words mean, let alone which I prefer! All I know is that Jesus is coming back. Isn't that all that matters? I know You'll take care of me no matter what.

I do admit that I wonder about the details. I wish I knew what will happen when You come and I wish I knew the day You'll come so I will be ready. I don't want to be in the shower or yelling at the kids when You come. Maybe that's part of Your plan—not knowing motivates me to live each moment so that I'll be proud for You to see what I am doing (vv. 2-4).

I read in 1 Thessalonians 5:4-7 that I'm a child of the light and of the day. I'm not to be involved in things of night or darkness. That makes more sense when I think about what people do during those times. Night is the time people sneak out, get drunk, drive crazy, meet secret lovers, hide what they're doing.

Darkness also reminds me of loneliness, anger, hopelessness, and sadness. Because I know You don't want those for me, I find it easier to avoid activities that lead to them. I can ask myself: "Do I want other people to see me doing this?" "Would I be proud for the light to be turned on me?" "Though this looks attractive now, will it lead to a dark end?" These questions help me evaluate what I do, think, and say. Thanks for that illustration, Lord.

I've heard people say that Christians have their heads in the clouds, that they don't know what real life is all about. I think *they're* the ones who are asleep. Christians are the only ones alert enough to live life because they're in touch with You, the source of life. Staying alert keeps my energy flowing. You help me understand the way people and events fit together. Thanks for giving your insight. You help me understand actions that solve problems rather than making them worse, words that heal rather than hurt, attitudes that bring joy rather than frustration.

Being alert also has a sad side: I see people's pain. I notice the power Satan has. I experience the battle of living the Christian life. But You help me handle this sadness. You prompt me to action. You motivate me to be part of the solution rather than part of the problem. You remind me that You are in control and that Satan cannot ultimately triumph.

Sometimes the word "self-control" makes me feel bound, inhibited, robotic. As I ponder it further, I realize that's not what you mean. Self-control means guiding myself toward the path that brings happiness. It leads to more freedom, not less. Controlling my emotions in the midst of a fight helps me say what I feel without destroying the other person. Controlling my tongue makes sure I keep the secret my friend entrusted to me.

It's good to know I've got faith, love, and hope of salvation to protect me from the arrows life hurls at me. It's hard to imagine any stronger armor. I do admit that locks on my doors and money in my bank account give me a measure of security. Does that mean I don't depend on You? I hope not. I know those things are weak compared to You. Thanks for being strong even when other things appear stronger. Thanks for giving me faith and love to protect my body and everything inside me: thoughts, hopes, dreams, relationships, feelings, understanding. Thanks for giving me the hope of salvation to protect my head. It's such a cozy feeling to know that You'll get me through whatever happens: illness or separation or emotional pain or physical pain or fear or persecution or disappointment. You're what I need to face the present and the future.

When You say You'll come like a thief, I know You're not coming to take anything from me. Rather You know Your plan all along, but I don't. Your coming will seem sudden to me. That doesn't have to scare me because I know You won't bring Your wrath. You'll keep me beside You forever, whether I'm dead or alive. That's a nice secure feeling. Thanks for loving me so much.

Danielle

🎔LIVING UNTIL JESUS COMES🎔

Memorize 1 Thessalonians 5:5-6 or 5:8 to remind yourself to see life events the way God sees them, by His light. Every time you see a light bulb, the sun, or other light source, repeat the verses.

****

Paul explained in verse 1 that the times and the dates of Jesus Christ's return are not available to us. Write a letter to God telling your feelings and thoughts about His coming "like a thief in the night." What do you like about not knowing when He will arrive? What makes you uneasy about it? Why would you rather know or not know the details? How are you comfortable or uncomfortable with leaving the details in God's hands? What are you most looking forward to about His return?

****

List everything you did yesterday. Which actions would you want another Christian to see you do? Which would you want God to see you do? These are actions of the light, actions we're proud to have shown.

List your plans for today. Shine God's light on them, talking with Him about which ones He wants you to keep and which He wants you to change.

****

The word translated "sleep" covers all sorts of moral permissiveness. It means "spiritual laziness and indifference." What moral sins do you tend to fall into when you are not alert? (Possibilities include gossip, overeating, drinking, criticism, negativism, overspending.) Write a letter to God discussing why you tend to "go to sleep" and actions He wants you to take to keep alert.

TO DETAILS

❧LISTENING TO GOD'S WORD❧

There are three dimensions to the Christian life: our relationship with God, our relationships with people, and our inner attitudes. Of course, our relationship with God is the primary dimension. As we let God transform the way we treat people outwardly and the way we think inwardly, we become like Jesus. This is the essence of sanctification: letting God make us like Jesus. In 1 Thessalonians 5:12-28, Paul gave specific suggestions for how to live our Christian commitment in all three dimensions of life.

Read 1 Thessalonians 5:12-28
1. As you read 1 Thessalonians 5:12-28, substitute your name for every "you" and add your name to phrases where "you" is implied (e.g., "Be joyful always, Karen"—v. 16). Choose the phrase that most:

Encourages you—

Frightens you—

Excites you—

Worries you—

Relates to your life—

Challenges you—

Motivates you to follow God—

Now mark each phrase to identify whether it:
  ◊ Deals with your inner thoughts, attitudes, and responses.
  ⟨⟩ Explains how to relate to people, especially in your church.
  ⌂ Tells you how to respond to God.

2. Name a Christian who works hard in your church or Bible study group. With what words and actions do you (or could you) demonstrate respect and regard for this person? (vv. 12-13)

How do you keep from putting this person on a pedestal?

3. Reread verse 14. Jot down the initials of someone you know who:

Is idle—

Is timid—

Is weak—

Tries your patience—

Write specific words you could say to:

Warn this idle person—

Encourage this timid person—

Help this weak person—

Show patience to the one who makes you impatient—

4. What action or attitude makes you want to "pay back wrong for wrong"? (v. 15)

How does seeking to "do good" (RSV, GNB) make it easier to avoid revenge? Why will "kindness" (NIV) work better than paying back wrong?

5. What's the difference between always being joyful and always wearing a smile? (v. 16)

6. One key to continual joy is continual prayer. To practice praying continually (v. 17), write a one-sentence prayer you could say inwardly:

While talking with a friend about a problem.

While preparing to teach a Bible study class or seminar.

While teaching that class or seminar.

When your child spills her milk on your freshly waxed floor.

When you're disappointed about ———————————————————.

When your friend or spouse goes through pain.

When you're delighted about ————————————————.

7. The most difficult things that the Thessalonians had to face were conflict in their church and persecutions by people outside their church. Name the two worst things that have happened to you over the last year:

Now name something you could (or did) thank God for in the midst of, or following each (v. 18):

What good does it do to give thanks to God?

8. Apparently some in the Thessalonian church were negating the work of the Holy Spirit in others. Name a way you have done this (v. 19).

With what words or actions could you encourage a fellow believer to say or do as the Holy Spirit has instructed her?

9. Notice that verses 20 and 21 go together. While we never want to neglect a genuine biblical teaching, we need to evaluate each teaching to be certain it's from God. Name two or three questions you could ask in order to test everything and hold on to the good:

10. Name at least ten kinds of evil in your community that affect you or your family. How does avoiding them (v. 22) contribute to their decline?

11. Look up "sanctify" (v. 23) in a Bible dictionary. Write its definition in your own words. (Recall *For Further Study* in session 4.)

How do verses 23-24 describe sanctify? Who are the key persons in the process of sanctification?

12. What affectionate greetings do Christians use today in place of the holy kiss? (v. 15)

What positive effect do these greetings have in your church?

13. What will be the effects of obeying Paul's commands in 1 Thessalonians 5:12-22? (Explain your answers.)

For Further Study: Use a Bible concordance to read several verses that include the phrase "in Christ." Notice how often "in Christ" occurred in the letters of Paul. Why do you think Paul liked this phrase so well?

❦ *LIFE EXAMPLES* ❦

Takers seem to outnumber the servers in most churches. Even when the cooperative members outnumber the troublemakers, the troublemakers seem to demand the bulk of the church's energy. Early churches had their share of troublemakers too. The main ones in the Thessalonian church were the idlers. These people apparently thought it was more spiritual to quit their jobs and await Jesus' return than to work. This sounded holy, but the idlers actually used their free time to meddle. Their unruliness and opposition to those who worked caused friction in the church.

Two other groups caused extra work for the Thessalonian church, though not as intentionally. The timid were anxious about their friends who had died (recall 4:13-18) and about their own salvation (recall 5:1-11). They were immobile rather than troublesome. They needed encouragement to live what they believed. They needed reminders of the truth, corrections of false teaching, and gentle prodding to express their spiritual gifts.

The weak (v. 14) were not physically weak but morally weak. They were easily tempted to participate in wrong activities, especially sins of a sexual nature (recall 4:3-8). They tended to return to their pagan lifestyles when things got rough. These persons needed tender, consistent support and accountability.

All three types of persons—the meddlesome idlers, the worried timid, and the morally weak—were genuine Christians. Paul urged the Thessalonians not to be vengeful or impatient with each other but to work toward one another's good.

In addition to these relational instructions, Paul suggested specific ways to continue their personal spiritual growth. Attending to these details would help not only individuals but the entire church family.

Who are the people in your church who meddle, worry, or give in to obvious moral sin? What are your initial inner and outer reactions to them (one of them may be you)? Write in your journal or in a letter your feelings toward the takers in your church.

How would Paul advise that you respond to these persons? Fretting and fuming do little good. Ridding your church of troublemakers results in a very small church—and you may be the next one to fall into sin. Paul advised attending to details—daily actions of kindness and love coupled with attention to personal spiritual discipline. These details make a difference. When each church member feels needed rather than idle, confident rather than timid, victorious rather than weak, the church can't help but grow in spiritual depth and in size of membership.

Being slow to anger and seeking the good of the other are not easy actions. But they can lead even the most persistent taker toward becoming a giver. Notice that to be patient is literally to be "long tempered." Working toward each other's good does not mean to continue to let people take, but to motivate them to give, to guide them toward greater spiritual maturity. In some cases it might mean teaching a taker how to become a server through apprenticing; in others it might mean talking or listening; in a few it might mean admonishing or correcting. As you decide how to attend to the details in your church, ask: What action would motivate this person to trust God and to live life by His guidelines?

Continue your journal entry or letter with actions you could take to turn your frustration over a church member into fruit, your anger into encouragement. Your actions can lead to your fellow church member becoming a more mature Christian and your entire church becoming more effective in recognizing and living God's will.

❦LIVING UNTIL JESUS COMES❦

Memorize 1 Thessalonians 5:15 or 5:16-18. Select the passage that speaks to an area in which you need to grow spiritually. Repeat it every day this week and think of a specific way to live it that day.

****

Using the letters of your first name, find actions you can do to demonstrate your commitment to Christ in both your inner life and your outer relationships. Each time you hear your name remember to do these "first-name actions." Example:

K ind always.
A void every kind of evil.
R espect and regard highly those who work hard in our church.
E ncourage the timid.
N obody pays back wrong for wrong.

****

Notice the phrase "in Christ Jesus" in verse 18. Because we are in Christ, we can do all the things commanded in verses 12-22. Reread the verses, adding "in Christ Jesus" after every command. What difference does this make in your attitude toward obeying these commands? In your confidence to obey them? In your understanding of His faithfulness to you? In your relationship to Jesus Christ?

****

Read the blessing in 1 Thessalonians 5:23-24, substituting your name for every "you" and "your." Read the blessing again, substituting the names of your church's "takers." (See Life Examples.)

CHAPTER EIGHT

Persevere

THROUGH PERSECUTION

❦ *LISTENING TO GOD'S WORD* ❦

By the time this second letter was written, about six months after the first, the Thessalonians had become discouraged by continual persecution. Non-Christians misunderstood them and ridiculed their faith. Jews living in Thessalonica were jealous of the Gentile Christians and stirred up controversy and trouble. Because of these problems and because of false teachings they had experienced, the Thessalonians no longer felt worthy to be included in God's kingdom. Paul addressed these concerns in this passage.

Read 2 Thessalonians 1:1-12

1. Recall that Paul began the Thessalonian church, was separated from them suddenly, sent Timothy to check on them, and then wrote the letter which became 1 Thessalonians. The Thessalonians' continuing persecutions and troubles may have motivated this second letter.

   Notice the word "our" in verse 1. Why do you think Paul used this word?

2. Paul was delighted with the Thessalonians' growth in faith and growth in love for each other (v. 3). How does the way Christians treat each other demonstrate their faith (or lack of it)?

Choose a person in your study group or church. Jot down some ways she has grown in faith or in demonstrating love. Tell the person what you have noticed.

3. How do you think the other churches responded when Paul boasted about the Thessalonians' perseverance and faith? (v. 4)

4. What is the "evidence that God's judgment is right"? (v. 5)

5. How can we distinguish suffering for the kingdom (v. 5) from other types of suffering?

6. In what two ways will God demonstrate his righteous judgment? (vv. 6-7)

Which will mean the most to you? Why?

7. Those who refuse to establish a relationship with God (vv. 8-9) often know about hell and jokingly speak of going there. Why do you think these people persist in ignoring God when they seem to know the consequences?

What might convince a person like this to respond to God? (If possible, think of a specific person you know.)

8. One penalty for not knowing God is being "shut out from the presence of the Lord" (v. 9). Why would this be painful for you?

Why would this be painful for someone who doesn't know Jesus?

9. Verses 10 and 12 explain that we can glorify Jesus in ourselves. "Glorify" means to bring positive attention to, to praise, to honor. How can the way we respond to trouble glorify Jesus? Give an example, using a specific trouble.

How can the way we live daily glorify Jesus? Name at least five ways you can glorify Jesus in your daily routine.

10. How does a Christian live who is worthy of the kingdom of God and worthy of God's calling? (vv. 5, 11) Describe or draw such a person.

11. Write at least three goals you have for your life. Which of these "are good purposes . . . and prompted by your faith"? (v. 11)

Talk your goals over with God, asking Him to bring your plans into harmony with His. Write down the insights God gives you as you talk with Him.

For Further Study: Using a concordance or Bible dictionary, trace the words *glory* and *glorify* throughout the Bible. Discover ways people in the Bible glorified the Lord. Follow their examples.

❧LIFE EXAMPLES❧

It doesn't seem fair. Just when I think I have one problem solved, another one arises. If it's not my neighbor laughing at my faith, it's job troubles. If it's not job troubles, one of my kids is facing false teaching. If it's not the kids, it's church conflict. Is there no end to my troubles?

Repeated misunderstanding, pain, persecution, and ridicule can get even the strongest person down. But as Christians we don't have to stay down. It's not wrong to feel discouraged and defeated, but with God on your side, it's certainly wrong to stay there.

What can we do about it? Consider these possibilities:

"Who does he think he is? He can't treat me that way. Just wait till I get him back!"

"What's the use? Talking never does any good, and if I raise a fuss he'll just take it out on my child. There's not a thing I can do about it."

Revenge and withdrawal are two ways to respond to persecution and trials. Perhaps the Thessalonians had considered or tried these. Maybe they discovered that revenge and withdrawal, though initially easy, perpetuate the problem.

The Thessalonians turned to a better way: perseverance. They decided that they could keep going longer than the problems. They responded to their troubles with greater faith. They decided that God was bigger than the problems. They learned to depend on His strength even when things seemed hopeless. They trusted Him even when they didn't understand. Paul praised them for this and encouraged them to keep on glorifying God in their actions (1:3-5).

Despite their outward perseverance and faith, the Thessalonians were somewhat less confident inwardly. They apparently wondered if God still loved them. Perhaps those who persecuted them planted these seeds of doubt: "If God really loved you, He wouldn't let these problems come to you." "Maybe He's punishing you for something!" Paul countered this false teaching by assuring the Thessalonians that their trials were evidence of God's presence, not a signal that He had departed.

Paul assured the Thessalonians that their trials would not continue forever. God would bring relief and return trouble to those who caused it. God was and is in control. Jesus Himself will return to end trouble and reveal His glory. Paul encouraged the Thessalonians to hang on until then, living in such a way that God's influence in their lives would be obvious.

Think about a persecution you are presently facing. Perhaps someone misunderstands your faith. Possibly your child is caught between the world's demands and God's principles. Maybe a problem threatens to harm your church. It could be that someone is teaching or living something that causes pain to someone you care about. Jot down your persecution here: _____ .

What actions can you take to persevere through persecution? Perseverance faces the opposition directly, trusting God to take care of the situation. Perseverance knows that Jesus is coming back. Perseverance knows that while we're seeking solutions and waiting for relief, God can turn troubles into opportunities to grow and express faith. Perseverance demonstrates that God is right.

Reread 2 Thessalonians 1:1-12 to discover ways to persevere, to trust God even in the most difficult situations. Write ways these actions suggested in 2 Thessalonians 1 apply to your persecution:

☐ Thank God for each other (v. 3).

☐ Notice the faith and love expressed by other believers (v. 3).

☐ Share with friends from other churches the good that is happening in your church (v. 4).

☐ Remember that living God's way demonstrates the rightness of His way (v. 5).

☐ Trust God for relief (v. 7).

☐ Marvel at Jesus (v. 10).

☐ Focus on contemplating good purposes and good acts (v. 11).

☐ Glorify God in your words and actions (v. 12).

Obedience and persistence are much more powerful than frustration and fear. The Thessalonians chose to respond to their trouble in ways that demonstrated and strengthened their faith. You can too.

"We pray this so that the name of our Lord Jesus Christ may be glorified in you, and you in Him" (2 Thes. 1:12a).

❧LIVING UNTIL JESUS COMES❧

Memorize 2 Thessalonians 1:12. Recall that to glorify God is to bring Him positive attention, to cast the spotlight on Him.

****

Underline all the good news in 2 Thes. 1:1-12. How can these truths encourage you in the midst of your troubles? Write a song, poem, or letter to yourself expressing this. Use several of the words you underlined.

****

Reread 2 Thes. 1:3. "Growing" and "increasing" are crucial characteristics of faith and love. Name a way your faith has grown since you first became a Christian. Name a way you've learned to increase your expression of love for others.

****

Think about a friend who is going through troubles. Pray for that friend at least once each day this week, that she may "persevere" (v. 4) and *"by His power . . . may fulfill every good purpose"* (v. 11).

CHAPTER NINE

❧ LISTENING TO GOD'S WORD ❧

What do you most look forward to about Jesus' return? How would you feel if you thought you had missed it? The Thessalonians were in precisely this position. They had encountered some false teaching that proclaimed that the Day of the Lord had arrived. They wondered if the events surrounding Jesus' return had already occurred. Paul countered their confusion with facts.

Read 2 Thessalonians 2:1-17

1. A main purpose of this second letter to the Thessalonians was to stop a rumor. According to verse 2 how had this rumor spread? Who was this supposed to have come from? What did it say?

2. What actions did Paul ask the Thessalonians to take in response to the false teaching they had heard? (vv. 2-3)

What is the difference between truly false teaching and simple disagreement between Christians? How could the actions you've listed above help you distinguish between them?

3. What two events must happen before the Day of the Lord? (v. 3)

4. Describe the man of lawlessness, according to verses 4, 9, and 10.

5. One reason this passage is confusing is that the Thessalonians knew some details that we don't know (v. 5). Explain what you think holds back the man of lawlessness (vv. 6-7).

Why did you identify it as you did?

6. Jesus' very presence is stronger than all the lawless one's demonstrations of power (v. 8). How would you describe this to someone who feels discouraged about the present influence of evil in her life? (CAUTION: Avoid pat answers—weave sensitivity throughout your words.)

7. Recall that Jesus warned against accepting miracles as proof of God's activity (Matt. 7:22-23; Rev. 13:14). How do you think you could tell the difference between a genuine and a counterfeit miracle? (v. 9)

8. Why would God send delusion? (HINT: Notice the progression from verse 9 to verse 12.)

9. What will be the consequence of someone choosing to follow deception? (vv. 10-12)

How might you communicate this to a nonbeliever in a way that would motivate him or her to get to know God rather than moving further away from Him?

11. Three words describe each believer: *loved, chosen, called* (vv. 13-14). Choose your favorite and tell why it motivates you to obey God.

12. Waiting for the Second Coming of Jesus is not something we're to do passively. It's a time of active obedience based on God's power. Name a way you:

Stand firm (v. 15)—

Hold to true teaching (v. 15)—

Let God encourage you (vv. 16-17)—

Let God strengthen you (vv. 16-17)—

13. Recall that God's daily work in us is the essence of sanctification (v. 13; 1 Thes. 4:3-4; 5:23). Thank God for His personal interest in you and His efforts to bring you joy. Write your prayer here:

For Further Study: Not much is said about the *rebellion* mentioned in 2 Thessalonians 2:3. Consult commentaries to discover other references to it in the Bible. Focus on characteristics identified by the Bible itself, not on human speculation.

Review your study of *sanctify* (chapter 4).

🍂 *LIFE EXAMPLES* 🍂

Why does evil have so much power? A Christian can be defeated by the smallest problem. When wicked people prosper in more obvious ways than Christians, we are tempted to try their ways. Why can't all our spiritual disciplines and trust in God protect us from the lure of sin?

The answer lies in delusion. Satan knows that it's easy to reject outright lies; so he takes truth and twists it. He tells half truths, leaving out the more important parts. This makes wrong look right and right look stupid.

Satan also makes us think that it doesn't really matter what you believe. This simply isn't true. A measure of disagreement among Christians is normal. However, certain differences indicate false teaching (e.g., Jesus is one of many Messiahs). The Thessalonians had been taught that the Day of the Lord had already occurred. This unsettled and alarmed them. Believing something that's not true leads to confusion, frustration, and anguish. Understanding and believing truth brings peace and happiness.

The best way to spot a counterfeit is to know the real thing. When you understand the Bible, you'll recognize twisted truth. Identify the delusion in each of these examples and replace it with God's truth. Samples follow each:

THE DELUSION: The main way to express love is through sex. This usually occurs on the first or second date. Married couples seldom have an exciting sex life, so marriage is not necessary. In the media, no one ever gets hurt by out-of-marriage sex—no one experiences emotional anguish, uses birth control, contracts a venereal disease, or gets pregnant (except on the soaps and nobody takes those seriously). Sexual relationships are easy come, easy go. There's no need for commitment. Free sex is exciting, pleasurable, and harmless.

THE TRUTH: The half truth is that sex is exciting and pleasurable. The other half is that marriage and commitment are necessary to keep it that way. True sexual freedom comes through commitment, not casualness. True sexual happiness requires the foundation of marriage. Sex tends to bind one person to the other and makes "easy go" impossible (Matt. 19:5-6). Sex creates more problems than it solves when expressed outside of marriage.

THE DELUSION: The American dream is the way to happiness. Happiness comes through a three-bedroom house, two cars, and a successful job.

THE TRUTH: The half truth is that we do need shelter, transportation, and meaningful work. The rest of the truth is that pleasing God is more important than these. We depend on God, not a prestigious neighborhood or stable job, for security and for the meeting of our materal and emotional needs. When we put material and emotional needs first, we stay frustrated. When we put God first, we find joy no matter how difficult (or easy) our material and emotional circumstances (Matt. 6:33).

THE DELUSION: Happiness comes through a problem-free life.

THE TRUTH: The half truth is that we do feel better when we aren't in the midst of a crisis, an illness, or a problem. The rest of the truth is that problems are part of life until Jesus comes back. Solving problems, not the absence of them, brings happiness. God can use problems to strengthen our understanding, our faith, our relationships (Rom. 8:28).

THE DELUSION: When things get bad, get away from it all through glamorous vacations, drinking, or drugs.

THE TRUTH: The half truth is that we do need a break from pressure. We need to take a sabbath—a weekly rest prescribed by God at creation. The rest of the truth is that escape doesn't solve problems. It just covers them up for a while. To solve stress, talk with God about what needs to be done and implement His plan. God offers the solution, not an escape (Phil. 4:13, 19).

Ponder other ways Satan deceives in your everyday life. Replace the counterfeit with the real thing: God's truth. Use these areas as idea starters:

Relationships	Marriage	Happiness
Church	Responsibility	Routine
Communication	Parenting	Commitment

✿ *LIVING UNTIL JESUS COMES* ✿

Memorize 2 Thessalonians 2:8 to remind yourself that Jesus will over-throw all evil. A day is coming when you and those you love will be safe. How does looking forward to that day make it easier to get through your troublesome days?

****

Read 2 Thessalonians 2:1-15 several times. As you read it imagine how you would have felt:
☐ When you heard the false teaching (vv. 1-3).
☐ When you heard Paul's truth (vv. 4-11).
☐ When you realized that because you are a Christian you will not be condemned (v. 12).
☐ When you noticed that God wants to encourage you and strengthen you to live His way (vv. 13-17).
Write your thoughts in your journal.

****

Write verses 16 and 17 on a card and make an attractive border around it. Send it to a Christian friend.

****

Name a situation in which you find it difficult to live your Christian commitment. Reread 1 Thessalonians 2:15. Talk with God about the strength you need to obey Him in this situation. Reread verses 16 and 17, realizing that God is the source of strength and encouragement.

CHAPTER TEN

Find Meaning

IN YOUR WORK

❧ *LISTENING TO GOD'S WORD* ❧

"The Lord knew what He was doing when He gave us work to do," said my wise aunt, pleased that she could resume her responsibilities after a debilitating illness. What are the advantages of work? What pleasures does it bring? What problems does it avoid? Notice the value of work as you study 2 Thessalonians 3.

Read 2 Thessalonians 3:1-18
1. Examine Paul's prayer requests in verses 1-2. How are they similar to and different from prayer requests you have made?

2. Paul recognized that because not everyone obeyed God, there would be problems. He requested prayer for himself as well as assuring the Thessalonians of God's same protection (vv. 2-3). Which do you think God does more often: give us strength to get through the evil situation *or* take the evil situation away? Why?

3. How do God's love and Christ's perseverance enable you to obey God? To handle encounters with wicked and evil men? (vv. 3-5) Give specific examples.

4. In verses 6-15 Paul returned to a problem introduced in 1 Thessalonians 5:14. What was the problem?

5. What problems had the idleness led to? (vv. 10-11)

Why do you think it persisted even after Paul requested its end in his First Letter of the Thessalonians?

6. Why did Paul work when it was his right to be paid as a minister of the Gospel? (vv. 7-10)

7. Paul's goal in reprimanding the idle was redemptive. Rather than reject them, he wanted to motivate them to mend their ways and turn to following God in this matter. Name words, phrases, or actions in verses 6-15 that indicated this:

Verse 6—

Verses 7-9—

Verse 12—

Verse 13—

Verse 15—

How might you use these same actions to redeem a troublesome person in your church or Bible study group?

8. "The people in our church that do the least seem to complain the loudest," confides your friend. How do you respond based on 2 Thessalonians 3:6-13?

9. What makes you tire of doing right? (v. 13)

What might help you continue? (Reread verses 4-5.)

10. What three actions did Paul suggest for those who did not heed his exhortation? (vv. 14-15)

Why did Paul emphasize that they were still brothers?

11. What words and actions would help motivate a wayward believer to mend her ways? (v. 14)

When does lack of association cause more damage than it helps?

12. How do you communicate that you are still sisters with someone who has disobeyed God in some way? (v. 15)

13. Think back through your last ten weeks of study. How has studying 1 and 2 Thessalonians refined your understanding of Jesus' return? Write three ways you can live for Jesus until He comes.

For Further Study: Read the closings in each of Paul's letters. What words are repeated again and again?

Review the words *grace* and *peace* using a Bible dictionary and a concordance to better understand why Paul emphasized them.

❧ LIFE EXAMPLES ❧

What do you do with your time? Whether you are paid for it or not, significant work makes an important difference in your life and the lives of those you touch. Several people in the Thessalonian church did not see work this way. They had stopped working for one or both of these reasons: (1) They were so confident of the immediate return of Jesus that they quit their jobs and did nothing but wait. If Jesus was coming back soon, work was not necessary; (2) They thought work was not spiritual enough to devote time to. They saw labor as degrading, something for slaves and hired hands. They failed to recognize it as an element of Christian discipleship.

These people were not just relaxing—they were loafing. They had ceased work and were imposing on others. They felt they demonstrated their faith by not working, but didn't mind eating the food of those who did work. Paul mentioned this problem in 1 Thessalonians 4:11 but because nothing had been done about it, he addressed it in more detail and with more firmness in 2 Thessalonians 3.

How did Paul suggest dealing with idleness? He firmly but lovingly commanded them to work. Then he instructed the working Christians to stay away from the idle ones. His goal was not to reject the idle but to give them an opportunity to look within and recognize the error of their ways. He wanted them to see that work was not a denial of God but a way to serve Him.

Paul pointed out the importance of work in four ways: First, he himself was an example, working to support himself even when he was entitled to ministerial pay (vv. 7-9). Second, he requested that the Thessalonians follow his model (v. 9). Third, he reminded the Thessalonians of a proverb he had taught them before: "If a man will not work he shall not eat" (v. 10). Fourth, he commanded the idle to settle down and earn their bread (v. 12).

What's good about work? Consider the following:

☐ Work can meet a need of specific people in your community.

☐ Work can contribute to the family pocketbook.

☐ Work can help others grow spiritually either through direct ministries or through relationships.

☐ Work provides a way to use your God-given talents.

☐ Work can give a sense of purpose.

☐ Working with others brings out your good and smooths off your rough edges.

☐ Work can be an avenue for demonstrating your love for God.

☐ Work can demonstrate the Christian lifestyle.

☐ Work can help you use your time well (Eph. 5:16-17).

Significant jobs are more than the 9-to-5 standard. Consider these alternative ways to work:

☐ Accept a weekly obligation at your church (e.g., teaching Sunday School, leading a youth Bible study; running errands for shut-ins; etc.).

☐ Spend time with your children.

☐ Counsel a friend.

☐ Work a paid part-time job during school hours.

☐ Volunteer at school or in the community.

☐ Develop a home-based industry, perhaps one in which your children, your spouse, or a friend are involved.

☐ Lead a Bible study.

☐ Discover needs in your church and meet them (e.g., provide meals for a shut-in; care for children when a parent is sick; type the church newsletter; freshen up a broken-down classroom).

☐ Pray.

☐ Listen to those who are brokenhearted or rejoicing (Rom. 12:15).

☐ Serve on a committee at your church that keeps things running smoothly, researches solutions, or keeps communication open.

☐ Be a peacemaker (2 Thes. 3:16).

The purpose of work is to use your time to glorify God. Far from being a menial task that we finish in order to get on with living the Christian life, work can be an avenue for serving God. It can include family, church, and financial commitments.

The opposite of work is time on one's hands. Extra time leads to such problems as: frustration, boredom, restlessness, a critical spirit, feelings of purposelessness, time to worry rather than trust God, irritability, and "busybody-ness."

The Thessalonians had fallen into this trap. Rather than being busy, they became busybodies (v. 11). Why does this happen? We want to fill our time so we end up filling it with nosiness and criticism. This is seldom intentional; it comes because we want and need to notice, understand, and discern. But without responsibility, we often create more problems than we solve.

Second Thessalonians 3:1-18 guides us to find and enjoy meaningful work, work that resists evil (vv. 2-3), depends on God (v. 5), does what is right (v. 13), and promotes peace (v. 16). How do your present responsibilities do this? Which might God want you to drop? To begin?

❧LIVING UNTIL JESUS COMES❧

Memorize 2 Thessalonians 3:4-5 to help you remember that God's love brings the strength you need to obey verse 13 and that Christ's perseverance is your example for doing so.

****

Write a letter to a fellow Christian who is disobeying God in some way. Follow the principles used by Paul in 2 Thessalonians 3. You will probably choose not to mail it; but let the letter help you work out words you might use in talking to this sister you love.

****

Now write a letter to yourself about a way you are disobeying God. Use the same loving principles. Read the letter to God thanking Him for His faithfulness and love. Ask God to help you be confident in and dependent on His power to help you obey Him.

****

Read 2 Thessalonians 3:13 in several translations. Choose the one you like best or paraphrase it in your own words. Write the verse and decorate it. Display it where you will see it daily.

❧LEARNING FROM OTHERS❧

Suggestions for Leading a Bible Study Group

☐ Realize that the study is in God's hands. Relax as you pray for His guidance and watch His truth come alive.

☐ Encourage members to complete the Listening to God's Word section before arriving. This helps discussion to be Bible-based.

☐ Encourage your members to read from their own Bibles, especially when translations vary. Explain that the New Testament was originally written in Greek and that Bible translators have studied the Greek and translated it into English. Because Greek is a much more precise language than English, it is difficult to translate it precisely. Thus, translators might word Bible truth differently. This variety enhances our understanding of God's word.

☐ Resist the urge to do most of the talking. Your role is that of facilitator. Your goal is to guide your group to share insights from the Bible, to steer them away from fruitless tangents (some tangents are worth pursuing!) and to give the members confidence in studying the Bible for themselves. Emphasize that God speaks to us through His Word. Encourage members to listen to Him rather than becoming overly dependent on commentaries or a human teacher.

☐ Welcome every contribution. "Good point!" "Right from the Scripture!" and "Excellent insight!" are a few of the phrases you might use. Even totally wrong answers can be affirmed with "You're close," or "I can tell you thought about that one!"

☐ Don't fear silence. You have thought about the questions all week but the other members may have just heard it. Silence gives them time to think about their answers. Try counting to fifteen to help you realize that the silent pauses are not as long as they seem.

☐ Balance contributions between shy and talkative members. Try these techniques: ask everyone's response to a certain question; introduce a "rule" that no one can answer two questions in a row; nod at hesitant members; direct more difficult questions to those with greater confidence and more obvious questions to timid members; assign a different question to each group member and provide time to prepare responses.

☐ As time allows, select features from the Living Until Jesus Comes section to supplement or close the Bible study session. Don't force members to share during this time but realize that sharing can provide opportunity to encourage each other to live God's way. Suggest that telling some of our decisions can make us accountable and more likely to follow through with them. Include a time of congratulations for commitments accomplished since the last session.

☐ As you lead a group studying 1 and 2 Thessalonians, you'll notice that every Bible study group has its own unique personality. As you get to know yours better, you'll discover which questions best encourage members to dig into the Scripture and which elicit the most conversation, the firmest conviction, the greatest life changes.

❧ LEADER'S GUIDE 1 ❧

Objective
To identify ways we can model Christian living in everyday life and to notice the Christian models around us.

Personal Preparation
☐ Read 1 Thessalonians 1:1-10 and an introduction to the Book of 1 Thessalonians. Many Bibles include an introduction at the beginning of each Bible book. If yours does not, look in a Bible dictionary or commentary.

☐ Study the introduction to this guide which overviews the Thessalonian letters. Underline points you want to make during this session.

☐ Read the "Suggestions for Leading a Bible Study Group" on the previous page. Star actions you plan to take.

Leading the Group
☐ Introduce the study of 1 and 2 Thessalonians, using the Introduction to this guide.

☐ Question 1. Refer members to the Introduction for help answering this question.

☐ Question 2. *Author:* The author was Paul. Timothy and Silas were included because they related to and were concerned for the Thessalonians too (notice "we" throughout the book). *Recipient:* Recall that "church" meant the people belong to the Lord, not the building. *Greeting:* Point out that Paul's greeting was different from the typical: It was distinctly Christian. "Grace" is God's love which He gives freely no matter what we've done. "Peace" is the well-being that comes from being one with Christ. Paul included both Greek and Jewish Christians by using "grace," the Greek greeting and "peace," the Jewish greeting.

☐ Question 4. As you discuss this question, note that the Thessalonians' "endurance" was not passive acceptance. It was positive, active, and mature. Endurance pictures a soldier who can sustain his opponent's attack yet reserve strength to win the final battle.

☐ Question 5. Explain that their suffering came because of their commitment to Christ and that joy in the midst of affliction characterizes true believers. One is never happy that the affliction comes but happy to have victory over it.

❧ *LEADER'S GUIDE 2* ❧

Objective
To notice and talk about the good in the ministers who lead us.

Personal Preparation
☐ Read 1 Thessalonians 2:1-16 several times. As you read it, ponder how Paul's leadership was like that of Jesus. Ponder how your leaders are like/unlike Paul.
☐ Star questions you want to spend the most time discussing.

Leading the Group
☐ Question 1. Encourage participants to identify the criticisms by studying Paul's responses. For example: "Our visit was not a failure" (v. 1) indicates that someone may have accused Paul of failure.

Explain that, at the time of this letter, traveling philosophers and religious teachers frequently exploited gullible people for financial gain. Perhaps jealous Jews accused Paul of the same insincerity, of being more concerned about making money than about presenting true teaching, or of other deceptive actions.

☐ Question 2. Encourage group members to give the reason for each phrase they chose.

☐ Question 5. Samples: Rather than authoritarian assertion, Paul led with gentleness and tenderness. He cared for and cherished his people. He shared his life ("practiced what he preached") rather than just talking about it. He refused to be condescending and spoke to them as brothers and sisters. He was loving. He refused to compromise on Christian standards, encouraging believers to live God's way.

☐ Question 9. Caution against anti-Semitism. Though many Jews misunderstood their mission, rejected Jesus Christ, brought His death and the death of His prophets, others accepted Jesus. Jesus Himself was a Jew. So was Paul. Explain that Jewish leaders thought Paul was a traitor for preaching to the Gentiles (Acts 17:5, 13). They thought Paul was disobeying God.

☐ Question 10. Example: A consequence of gossip is the breakdown of trust between friends which creates loneliness.

☙ LEADER'S GUIDE 3 ☙

Objective
To discover and take deliberate actions to encourage fellow believers during separation or other difficult times.

Personal Preparation
☐ Read 1 Thessalonians 2:17–3:13 several times. As you read it underline words, actions, and attitudes that Paul used to deal with his separation from the Thessalonians.

☐ Read Paul's blessing in verses 11-13. What blessing would you like to give each Bible study member?

Leading the Group
☐ Question 1. You may want to assign the three roles (converted Jew; jealous Jew; Paul) to different Bible study members. Encourage them to talk among themselves to help each other understand the different points of view. Ask: What similar situations do we face today? What actions might God recommend?

☐ Question 2. Note that Paul wanted the Thessalonians to know that the separation was not his choosing (v. 17). The jealous Jews may have used Paul's absence as still further "proof" that he didn't really care for the Thessalonians (recall 1 Thes. 2:1-16).

☐ Question 3. The "crown" stood for victory or success. Rather than a metal item with jewels, it was a festive garland or wreath awarded to the winner of a game. Because a crown was the visible reminder of victory, the Thessalonian believers would be living demonstrations of the effectiveness of Jesus Christ. They were Paul's pride and joy and will be tangible reasons to celebrate victory when Jesus Christ comes in glory.

☐ Question 4. Explain that "we" is Paul and Silas. Paul sent Timothy because he was unable to come himself.

☐ Question 5. Point out that some Christians turn away from God during times of trouble, angry that He caused or permitted them. Recognizing that persecutions are not God's idea, but Satan's, helps us realize that God is on our side. Tolbert points out that this is the essence of the temptation Paul speaks of: to turn away from God because trusting Him didn't do any good. Paul was worried that the Thessalonians' trials may have placed them in this dangerously vulnerable position.

☐ Question 9. If time allows, direct members to write a blessing for the person on their left using the blessing activity suggested under Living until Jesus Comes. Provide paper on which to write the blessings.

🍂 *LEADER'S GUIDE 4* 🍂

Objective
To notice ways we already delight God and to pinpoint daily actions that would please Him more completely.

Personal Preparation
☐ Read 1 Thessalonians 4:1-12 several times. As you read it meditate on God's good gifts of sexuality, relationships, and work. Praise Him for these good gifts and ask for insight to express them the way He wants you to.

☐ Ask God to work in each member's life (including your own) to convict, counsel about the next action, and comfort them with unconditional love.

Leading the Group
☐ Question 1. Encourage members to list what they are already doing as well as what they'd like to be doing. When we begin with ways we already please God, we feel encouraged toward more perfect obedience, rather than feeling defeated. Notice Paul's admonition in verses 9-10. He first pointed out ways the Thessalonians love each other and then encouraged them to love more and more.

☐ Question 4. Samples: because we know God (v. 5); because it hurts other people (v. 6); because God has called us to be pure (v. 7).

Explain that in the first century, sexual standards were similar to today's: Sexual sin was condemned but few took God's laws seriously enough to obey them. Most felt that abstinence before marriage and sexual loyalty within marriage were unrealistic expectations. "Not like the heathen" (v. 5) insisted that guidelines for sexual behavior be taken from God, not from society.

☐ Question 5. Examples include: Extramarital sex often leaves at least one partner feeling "used"; Adultery betrays the trust and happiness of marriage relationship; Pregnancy is possible even with birth control; Can transmit AIDS and other venereal diseases; Causes one to lose respect.

☐ Question 9. Encourage members to think about specific needs in their church, home, job, and community.

☐ Question 10. Suggest that living quietly does not mean to refuse to share your faith, nor does it mean inactivity. It depicts those with inner peace who are free to love and give rather than take and accuse.

Point out that some Thessalonian Christians were so certain that Christ would return soon that they quit working and relied on others to support them. Without work they had plenty of time to meddle in people's affairs.

❧ *LEADER'S GUIDE 5* ❧

Objective
To recognize the certainty of the Christian hope of life after death and to experience the difference that hope makes in our grieving.

Personal Preparation
☐ Read 1 Thessalonians 4:13-18 from several translations. Each translator had unique insight into the meaning of the Greek words and so adds depth to our understanding of the Bible.
☐ Review one of your own grief experiences as guided by the second suggestion under the Living until Jesus Comes feature. Prepare to share it with the group during the closing.

Leading the Group
Introduce the study by calling on two volunteers to read the conversation between Gina and Beverly. Ask: What do you think about Gina's words? About Beverly's feelings? After several have responded, explain that Beverly's feelings are very normal and very godly. As Paul explained in 1 Thessalonians 4:13-18, we grieve, but not as those who have no hope. Jesus Himself is our hope. Because Jesus is coming back, we know that every Christian will rise from death and live with Him forever. But in the meantime, we miss our loved ones. That's OK.
☐ Question 1. Briefly explain the meaning of grief and helpful ways to grieve using Life Examples.
☐ Question 4. Note that our confidence about life after death is based on historical fact: Jesus Christ rose from death.
☐ Question 7. As members share their images, encourage them to focus on specific words in the passage such as "loud command," "archangel," "trumpet call," "caught up," "clouds," "meet the Lord," "in the air."
If Bible study members find it helpful, supplement with these images suggested by Bible commentators (*after* they have shared theirs):
*The word translated "meet" is a Greek noun used to describe the public welcome given to important visitors by a city. We Christians will give our Lord a grand public welcome.
*Because Paul's listeners believed that the air was the home of the demons, there may be significance to meeting in the air. Meeting His believers in the air would demonstrate Jesus' mastery over the demons.
☐ Closure. As time allows, share personal grief experiences as guided by the Living until Jesus Comes feature. After each, ask: How can (or did) Jesus give hope through this?

❦LEADER'S GUIDE 6❦

Objectives
To name several ways to live as a person of the light and to realize that living for Jesus is one of the best ways to watch for Him.

Personal Preparation
☐ Read 1 Thessalonians 5:1-11 several times. As you read it ponder what it means to live as a child of the light and of the day.

☐ To help with question 9, bring a breastplate and helmet or a picture of one (pictorial Bible dictionaries and Sunday School teaching pictures are two possible sources). Read about each and what they were used for in Bible times.

Leading the Group
☐ Question 3. Encourage members to explore the illustration with several descriptive words such as: "deliberately," "unexpectedly," "with purpose in mind," "without you noticing at first," "quietly." A sample longer description: Even though the thief may have been planning his arrival for a long time (as has God) we notice his arrival suddenly.

☐ Question 5. You may want to suggest that though Christ will come suddenly for both believers and nonbelievers, only nonbelievers will be surprised. Believers know He is coming, so we're watching for Him.

Invite those who have borne children to tell how they prepared for labor. Ask: **If you have borne one or more children, how did you prepare for labor even though you did not know when it would come? (e.g., preregistered at the hospital, arranged for neighbors to be on call to take care of older children, took classes, etc.) How was actual labor different from what you expected? Would you rather have known or not known what it would be like? Why? How was the way you handled labor similar to the way you think you'll handle the Lord's return? Different from it?**

☐ Question 9. Suggest that Bible study members ponder the body parts these armor pieces protect, how these pieces function, what would happen without them. Motivate multiple comparisons between these and faith, love, and hope of salvation.

☐ Question 12. Point out that many of us find it difficult to encourage or to receive encouragement. Ask: **What makes it hard? What makes it worth overcoming the uneasiness to encourage anyway?**

Reread the last phrase of verse 11, "As in fact you are doing." Encourage your group to notice the ways they already encourage each other and build from there.

❧LEADER'S GUIDE 7❧

Objective
That each member select at least three actions from 1 Thessalonians
5:12-28 to attend to details in her life. One action will deal with inner
details, one with human relationships, and one with her relationship
with God.

Personal Preparation
  ☐ Read 1 Thessalonians 5:12-28 several times. As you read it underline
the actions you most need to take. Star the one you plan to work on first.
  ☐ Notice that this passage is highly application-oriented.

Leading the Group
  ☐ Question 1. Call for each member to name one command and how
she can apply it in her life. Notice that some actions can apply two or more
ways. For example: "Be joyful always" is at first glance an inner life action.
It can also be a relationship-to-God action because communicating with
Him brings the joy. It could even be a human relationship action because
friends could notice your joy and be encouraged by it.
  ☐ Question 2. Explain that "respect" means to know well enough to
understand and appreciate the worth of. "Admonish" means to correct, to
get back on the right track.
  ☐ Question 4. Agree that vengeance is a normal human reaction but
that it usually perpetuates the problem. Encourage group members to
suggest kind words and acts (NIV) or ways to "do good to one another" (RSV,
TEV, TLB versions) that tend to stop the problem rather than perpetuate it.
Point out that there is a difference between kindness and being spineless.
  ☐ Question 8: This question prevents gossip about others' sins by focusing on one's own. It also ends positively by naming ways to encourage the
Holy Spirit's work rather than stifle it.
  ☐ Question 9: Explain that "prophecy" is not predicting the future but
teaching the truth as guided by God. This occurs frequently in sermons or
talks but can also occur in casual conversation. Thus to quench the Holy
Spirit could mean to keep from saying or doing something God wants you
to say or do.
  ☐ Review. To review 1 Thessalonians 5:12-28, guide Bible study members to complete the first-name exercise suggested under "Living until
Jesus Comes." Provide paper. When the exercise is completed, call for each
member to read their "first-name actions."

❧ *LEADER'S GUIDE 8* ❧

Objective
To recognize how trusting God to bring about His present and future purposes makes it easier to persevere in trouble.

Personal Preparation
☐ Read 2 Thessalonians 1:1-12 several times. As you read it ponder troubles through which you and your Bible study members are traveling. Pray for clear insight into the meaning of troubles.
☐ Identify at least one godly characteristic in each person in your group for which you are especially thankful.

Leading the Group
☐ Question 1. Suggest that the word "our" emphasized that Paul and the Thessalonians were brothers and sisters and thus shared similar experiences, both trials and pleasures, of Christianity.
☐ Question 2. Guide your Bible study members to tell each other ways each has grown in faith and ways each demonstrates love. Agree that it is difficult to accept such affirmation, but affirmation can encourage us to live faith and show love "more and more" (Heb. 10:24-25). Emphasize that the source of these good things is God.
☐ Question 3. Point out that Paul's boasting was likely meant to encourage other churches. Ask: Would there have been jealousy? How can our admiration of other people's faith result in motivation rather than competition?
☐ Question 4. It's not easy to discover the exact identity of the "evidence." Encourage Bible study members to read and reread this first chapter of 2 Thessalonians to let the Scripture identify the evidence.
☐ Question 6. Enhance discussion by asking: How does knowing that God's judgment is coming make it easier to persevere during trouble?
☐ Question 7. At first glance, verse 8 seems rather harsh. Would it be fair to punish people who had never heard of God? No. The words "do not know God" refer to people who have heard of God but refuse to accept Him. "Know" means to establish close relationship with, to be intimately related with, to obey the Gospel, to accept Jesus. Thus those who "do not know God" hear this truth but refuse to heed it.
☐ Question 9. Point out that Jesus' name is His whole self, not just a label.
☐ Question 10. Explain that worthiness involves a new type of conduct and is demonstrated through these new actions and attitudes.

❧ LEADER'S GUIDE 9 ❧

Objective
To depend on God's encouragement and power rather than worrying over false teachings about Christ's second coming.

Personal Preparation
☐ As you study 2 Thessalonians 2, notice that Paul spends more time discussing encouragement (vv. 1-3, 5-6, 8, 13-17) than the power of Satan and the man of lawlessness (vv. 3-4, 7-8, 9-12). In fact just about the time the description gets scary, Paul interspersed a reminder of Christ's power (see v. 8).

Leading the Group
☐ Question 1. The rumor was that the Day of the Lord had come. This day would include several events, including the coming of Jesus Christ.
Point out 3:17 where Paul validates that this letter contained the truth from him, not the former rumors.
☐ Question 3. Explain that a rebellion is a deliberate opposition and voluntary defiance of God. Christians have called it the apostasy or the religious revolt.
Point out that some believers equate this man of lawlessness with the Antichrist. Others simply call him the "son of destruction," the "man of sin," or the "son of perdition" (literally "man doomed to destruction"). Whoever he is, he opposes God in every way, refusing to be ruled by Him. Verses 3 and 6 explain that he will be revealed at the proper time.
☐ Question 5. Point out that equally sincere Christians think the one who holds back could be God, a human empire or power, the Gospel of Jesus Christ, the order of the universe, or Satan (in this case the word might be translated "hold fast").
☐ Question 6. Explain that "mystery" ("secret" in some translations) in the Bible indicates something which is to be kept secret until a specific time. It's not a puzzle to be solved.
☐ Question 9. State that God wants everyone to love Him and His truth. But if they refuse (v. 10), He lets them believe what they want to (v. 11) and receive the consequences they choose (v. 12). The deceit comes to those who have already chosen to reject God. Refer members to Romans 1:24-32 for a picture of the progression of sin.
☐ Question 11. Point out the transition from focusing on the future of nonbelievers to focus on the future of believers. Invite any who have not yet become Christians to do so.

❧ *LEADER'S GUIDE 10* ❧

Objectives

To discover one or more ways each can work for God in her own life.
To review 1 and 2 Thessalonians, pulling together significant truths.

Personal Preparation

☐ As you read 2 Thessalonians 3:1-18, underline the points you most want your Bible study members to grasp. Notice the questions that deal with these passages and plan to spend the most time on them. Consider adding questions of your own.

☐ Review this study guide, highlighting truths you want to review. Plan to point these out as you discuss question 13. Perhaps you'll want to suggest that members circle these truths in their books or write them inside the front covers of their books.

Leading the Group

☐ Question 3. Point out that verse 5 gives specific suggestions for living the Christian life, "heart" standing for the entire inner life. Emphasize that God is always stronger than evil. Because He is also faithful and loving, we can depend on Him for confidence and strength to obey God no matter how many evil people oppress us (vv. 3-4).

☐ Question 5. They habitually depended on others for a living. They used their free time to meddle in each other's affairs and to stir up trouble. Perhaps the problem continued because well-meaning Christians kept on feeding and taking care of them which kept them from being motivated to work.

☐ Question 6. Supplement with these points: (1) Paul wanted to be an example. (2) Paul's critics had been saying that he preached for the money. Perhaps not taking pay would quiet these critics.

Emphasize that this passage taught the value of paying Christian servants, but that Paul chose to waive that right for specific reasons.

☐ Question 7. Examples: Paul used "brother" to address them (vv. 6, 15); He reminded them of past teaching (v. 6); He let his own life be an example = He was "a model for you to follow" (vv. 7-9); He used "urge" and addressed them directly (v. 12); He gave a positive goal (v. 13); He warned not to "regard him as an enemy" (v. 15).

☐ Question 10. He suggested three actions: (1) That they designate him as a troublemaker; (2) That they refrain from associating with him with the goal that he would be shamed, or look within and discover the foolishness of his action, repent, and mend his ways; (3) That they not regard him as an enemy but as a brother.

☐ Question 12. Agree that church discipline is hard. It's easier to become censorious and harsh than redemptive. Encourage tenderness and genuine concern for the well-being of offender, perhaps putting oneself in her place.